TIPS

to make

Good Group Decisions

Volume 1: The First Sixty

by
Craig Freshley

published by

Good Group Decisions, Inc.
2006

TIPS
to make
Good Group Decisions

Volume 1: The First Sixty

Copyright © 2006 Craig Freshley

Please review pages at the end of this book for our licensing agreement and reproduction guidelines.

For ordering information,
please see pages at the end of this book.

Front cover photo credit: www.e-Cobo.com
Back cover photo credit: Sarah Dubay

Manufactured in the United States of America

10 9 8 7 6 5 4 3 2 1

Published by
Good Group Decisions
98 Maine Street
Brunswick ME 04011
www.GoodGroupDecisions.com

Good Group Decisions is a registered trademark.

ISBN: 978-0-9788657-0-2

With gratitude for my Mom and Dad
and all my other teachers.
Thank you.

Contents

Purpose of this Book
What is a Good Group Decision?
About the Author
About the Tips

Act As If	1
Admit Mistakes	2
Agenda Setting Access	3
Assumptions Lead to Trouble	4
At Home and In Families	5
Best Solutions Begin with Self	6
Carrots Are Better Than Sticks	7
Change or Accept	8
Changing the Process is Rarely the Solution	9
Consensus Does Not Mean Casual	10
Consensus for Enduring Decisions....Only	11
Decide How to Decide	12
Define the Edges	13
Demonstrate Listening	14
Direction More Important Than Pace	15
Do What Say	16
Fertile Soil Helps Creativity	17
Freedom of Speech	18
Good in Everyone	19
Good Information Makes Decisions Self-Evident	20
Gratitude	21
Ground Rules	22
Head, Heart, and Hands....All Three	23
Humility	24
If It Fits In My Head, It Is Probably Too Small	25
If You Don't Have a Stake, Get Out of the Way	26
Interests Rather Than Positions	27
Kindness	28
Last Minute Decision Making	29
Listen	30

Love	31
Make Others Look Good	32
More Wagging, Less Barking	33
My First Thought is Probably Not My Best	34
Name Leads	35
No Complaining Without Contribution	36
Not Her Fault, Her Type	37
Outside Issues	38
Plan, Meet, Write-Up	39
Pose Alternatives	40
Putting People in Boxes is Not Okay	41
Reflective Pause	42
Resentments Have Roots in Expectations	43
Rules First	44
Separate Inputs from Outcomes	45
Separate Process from Program	46
Shared Expectations Minimize Conflicts	47
Shared Values	48
Shared Vision Required	49
Speak Your Truth and Let Go of the Outcome	50
Straw Vote	51
Structure Sets You Free	52
Take a Step	53
Talk or Listen	54
Understand First	55
Understanding and Trust, Both Required	56
Us Over Me	57
What's the Problem?	58
Write On the Walls	59
Written Words Clarify	60

Our Licensing Agreement with You
Order More Copies of This Book
Subscribe to Tips
About our Company

Purpose of this Book

The purpose of this book is to answer questions such as:

1. How do we make decisions in groups that **move toward peace**, where happiness and prosperity are increased among the people of the group?

2. How do we make decisions in groups that result in **environmental sustainability**, where long term effects are considered and negative impacts on the Earth are minimized?

3. How do we make decisions in groups that result in **corporate and organizational productivity**, where decisions are made efficiently and bring future returns in the form of future profits and/or saved costs?

4. How do we make decisions in groups **on behalf of the public**, where our governments make good policy choices on the best available data and in the interests of the group as a whole?

The tips and principles in this book are based on the idea that if you have good group process, you improve your chances of making good group decisions.

The tips and principles in this book apply to government decision makers, corporate and non-profit boards, business management teams, neighborhood groups, faith-based organizations, and others.

This book is useful to meeting facilitators, team leaders, executive directors, managers, elected officials, and board members.

This book is for anyone who wants to help their group make good decisions.

Tips to make Good Group Decisions, Volume 1   Freshley

What is a Good Group Decision?

Good group decisions endure and serve us well. We look back on such decisions with satisfaction knowing we did the right thing.

We measure the worth of a group decision by looking at the value of benefits gained or costs saved as a direct result of the decision. We also look at the cost of the decision making process; how much time it took, how much money, and other costs. We look at the ratio of these two things: benefits to costs.

Over the long run, good group decisions have more benefits than costs.

Results of Good Group Decisions

1. New, real benefits
As a result of the decision, problems are solved and/or quality of life is improved. People have new enthusiasm for working together. In a profit environment, groups make more profit. In a non-profit social environment, society is improved as a result of the decision.

2. Better relations
As a result of the decision, people get along with each other better. People are more peaceful toward each other. People communicate with each other with respect and efficiency, with fewer misunderstandings.

3. High efficiency
The decision making process is highly efficient and values people's time. The process of making good group decisions is not a waste of time. Group facilitation techniques are used to improve efficiency.

Ingredients for Good Group Decisions

Making good group decisions requires more than good group mechanics. Many groups are well-facilitated and move methodically through decision making steps, yet still make bad group decisions.

There are many how-to manuals for groups, but how the group behaves "as a group" is only one of three key ingredients. Good group decisions also depend on the attitudes of the decision-makers, and they also need to be acted on.

Good group decisions require three key ingredients:

1. As a Group
To make good group decisions, the group must have a shared vision, common values, and shared understanding of how decisions are made. There is order and respect for group process. Facilitation of the process is best separated from decision making about the issues.

2. Attitudes
To make good group decisions requires certain beliefs and attitudes of the participants. What people believe in their hearts matters. There are spiritual principles that, if we do not embrace them, we are not as likely to make good group decisions.

3. Actions
Decisions do not result in anything actually changing unless there is action; that is, somebody doing something more than talking or listening. Deciding is not enough. We have to actually do what we decided to do.

About the Author

I feel fortunate to have made a career out of studying how groups make decisions. I graduated from high school with honors in history, studied political science and philosophy in college, and studied public policy and management in graduate school.

I have worked for Maine state government in the field of natural resources policy development and I have worked for a non-profit organization on statewide economic analysis and downtown revitalization.

In 2003 I started a consulting company called Good Group Decisions. We facilitate meetings, offer training, and help groups with strategic planning and organizational development.

I have written another book which is soon-to-be-published: *Principles of Good Group Decisions*.

I am a Quaker, live in a Cohousing community, and I am on the board of directors of a Waldorf school. I am married and I have two children. Learn more about me and my company at www.GoodGroupDecisions.com.

About the Tips

I have sat through a lot of meetings in my career. Often frustrated, sometimes bored, I often jotted notes about how things could be better. I have been making notes, in the moment, for 15 years.

In 2003, I focused on writing and I compiled all my notes into a reference guide called *Principles of Good Group Decisions..*

In July, 2004 I began e-mailing one-page Tips to willing subscribers, about one every two weeks. I also posted them on my website. I got my ideas for the Tips from the meetings I was facilitating and from the reference guide I had written.

Many of the Tips are about individual beliefs. They are about attitudes, relationships, and philosophy. Some beliefs are helpful to group decision making, and some are not. Herein are Tips about helpful beliefs and attitudes.

Many of the tips are about individual actions and behaviors. Some behaviors are helpful to group decision making, and some are not. Again, herein are Tips about helpful behaviors.

Many of the Tips are for the group as a whole and their facilitators. They are group process suggestions. Herein are Tips about managing groups.

All the various types of Tips in this book are mixed together. None is more important than any other. They are not complete.

The Tips are like tips of icebergs. They are just tips.

Act As If

In principle, making good group decisions is really hard, a lot harder than making bad decisions. Making peace is much harder than making war. Getting along with each other and making good, lasting decisions takes a lot of practice.

"Act" is part of the word "practice." We do not get better without action. We do things poorly until we can do them well. It is not so important that we succeed, but that we try.

Practical Tip: Practice the principles of good group decisions as best as you can. For guidance ask yourself, "What would a peaceful person do?" Do not just talk about how to make peaceful decisions, or read about it, or think about it, but practice making good group decisions. Most of us are not very good peacemakers; but when we try to act as if we were, our world becomes more peaceful.

Admit Mistakes

In principle, we know we are prone to make mistakes; it is part of being human. And we know that mistakes are our best teachers. Learning from small mistakes prevents big mistakes later. Yet we are prone to cover up our mistakes, especially in our groups, and make a mess of things.

Good group decisions require humility among group members. I serve my group when I say, "I don't have all the answers and I don't do everything right;" and when I say, "It's okay for others to not be perfect."

Accepting that we are not perfect frees us to move on from mistakes without burden. Admitting mistakes helps us learn from them and let go of them.

Practical Tip: Be on honest watch for mistakes, perhaps a regular evening recount of the day's successes and mishaps. Try to isolate your mistakes from the mistakes or behaviors of others. Ask, "What was MY part?" In the case of a mistake made, admit your mistake to yourself and at least one other person. If an apology or amend is in order, do it.

Humility lightens our load and our outlook.

Agenda Setting Access

In principle, if we are a group of relative equals deciding how we are going to spend our time together it should be a group decision; or at least the group should decide the agenda setting process. Further, every member of the group should understand the agenda setting process and have access to it. In many groups, agenda setting is closely guarded by the majority or the chair and is often used to limit opposition. In most political systems, being able to control the agenda is a huge source of power.

Practical Tip: Establish an open and fair process for setting meeting agendas and make sure everyone knows the process. To maximize creativity, air all perspectives, share power and make it relatively easy for any new issue or idea to get at least a brief hearing. Some groups reserve a special time in every agenda where anyone can raise any issue, sometimes called Open Forum, and then the issue might be sent to committee or placed on a future agenda. Some groups vote or consent to approve the proposed agenda at the start of every meeting.

In any event, agenda setting is not trivial and if the agenda setting process is not formalized and widely understood in your group, it is likely limiting your creativity and your ability to make good group decisions.

Assumptions Lead to Trouble

In principle, there are three ways of knowing about something or someone: what we know, what we don't know, and what we think we know. It is usually what we think we know that gets us in trouble. When we assume things, we gamble; the bigger the assumption, the bigger the risk.

In any endeavor based on assumptions we can absolutely count on some of them giving way, like support timbers under a house collapsing. Some assumptions may hold for a long time, some almost forever, but most will collapse at a bad time and cause damage. When we make decisions based on facts and when we acknowledge all that we do not know, the long term outcomes are better.

Practical Tip: When analyzing a situation write down what you know, what you don't know, and what you assume. Naming assumptions is key. Want to play it safe? Do not make assumptions. How? Catch yourself making assumptions.

At Home and In Families

In principle, 90% of disease prevention and cure is done at home and in families. We all practice health care. We help each other eat well, get rest, and we take care of each other when sick. Only sometimes do we see a doctor or some other medical professional. Same with good group decisions: 90% of conflict prevention and resolution is done at home and in families. We help each other see things differently, we settle arguments, and we offer compassion and advice to those in conflict. Similarly in our jobs and in community groups; we all do the work of good group decisions. Only sometimes do we hire a professional facilitator or mediator.

Practical Tip: Just as you take 90% responsibility for your own health and your family's health, take 90% responsibility for peace and good decision making in the groups to which you belong. To do it well, educate yourself about what really works, beyond wives' tales, and try to actually do what you learn. Also, self-diagnose. Ask yourself, "What did I do today that contributed to a more peaceful world?" And, "How could I do better?" And like a sick person visualizing themselves as healthy, try to see yourself as a peacemaker. You do not need a professional license to practice.

Best Solutions Begin with Self

In principle, when things are not right, a natural instinct is to want someone else to do something different or to want a policy to be different. Rarely are these the best solutions. It is easy to think that my problem would be solved if only you would change. It is easy to think that the law or policy is wrong, rather than me. Sometimes laws or other people's attitudes or behaviors need to change, but it is often easier and more effective to change my own attitudes or behaviors.

Practical Tip: Before going to the governors of your group and suggesting a change in policy, or before going to another group member and suggesting they should change, ask yourself, "What is my part in this? What can I change about my own attitude or behavior to fix things?" After you have answered those questions, acted on the answers, and still things are not right; then ask your group or fellow group member to consider a change.

When we work to change a governing policy to fix an isolated problem, it can be hugely inefficient for many people. When we work to change the behaviors of others without willingness to change ourselves, it can take huge amounts of energy and result only in damaged relations.

To help the efficiency of good group decisions the first question is not, "What should he or she or they do to make things better?" but rather, "What am I going to do to make things better?"

Carrots Are Better Than Sticks

In principle, you can get a donkey to move forward in two ways: entice her in front with a carrot or hit her from behind with a stick. Carrots are rewards, incentives, appreciation, and – the most compelling – visions of how things can be better. Sticks are punishments, criticisms, and – the most destructive – defeatism, pessimism, and a sense that things are hopelessly bad. When motivated by sticks we are generally resentful, in pain, and when the stick is gone our motivation disappears. When we are motivated by compelling visions, it is called "inspiration" and it fuels our forward movement from within.

Practical Tip: Develop, nurture and share visions of things being better. Inspire! Rather than catch someone doing something wrong and criticize them, catch someone doing something right and praise them. Rather than focus on what bad things might happen if decided a certain way, focus on what good things might happen if decided differently. Good group decisions dwell in the realm of "good." Rather than complain about all that is wrong, give thanks for all that is right. Pass the carrots, please.

Change or Accept

In principle, when I am in conflict with others in my group or troubled by a difficult circumstance and I want relief, I have basically two choices. I can either work to change things for the better or I can work to accept things as they are. Both paths require effort on my part. Idle complaints, criticisms or gossip will not help things and will more likely make things worse.

It is helpful to keep in mind that I probably cannot change most things. The only thing I really have power over is my own beliefs and behaviors. If I changed my beliefs and behaviors would it ease the conflict?

Practical Tip: When in conflict, draw a circle around yourself. Draw it so that inside the circle are the things you can change and outside the circle are the things you cannot change. Step one: define the circle. Step two: work to change things within the circle. Step three: let go of all that is outside the circle. In other words: define your part; take responsibility for improving your part; do not take on other parts.

Work inside the circle – addressing the things you can change – is all about action. It's about doing things differently. Work outside the circle – the things you cannot change – is all about acceptance. It's about seeing things differently.

Changing the Process is Rarely the Solution

In principle, making good decisions together as a group requires three key ingredients: good process, the attitudes of individual participants, and the actions they take. What individuals believe and what they actually do in and outside of meetings matters. You can change the process to the point of perfection, but if the attitudes and actions are at fault, results will not change.

Practical Tip: Use individual conversations to address individual issues. Realize that for many problems encountered by your group, the problem is not the group's process. Problems are often the result of individual beliefs or behaviors. People often try to adjust group process as a backdoor way to address someone's different beliefs or to get someone to change their behavior. Changing group policy often seems easier than having a one-on-one conversation, but one-on-one conversations save group time and energy, and are often most effective at changing results.

Consensus Does Not Mean Casual

In principle, consensus generally means that all perspectives are heard and all concerns are addressed resulting in decisions to which all participants can willingly consent. Many groups aspire to make decisions by consensus, but very few have specific protocols in place to guide its implementation. There are no "Robert's Rules of Order" for consensus. Groups often plunge ahead resolved to use "consensus" but with little or no structural underpinnings.

Practical Tip: If you are going to use consensus as your official decision making method, be specific at the outset about what it means for your group. How, specifically, will you make sure that all perspectives are heard, all concerns are addressed, and what steps will be followed when there is a "block." Once decided, follow your rules with a degree of formality.

Structure and protocol is just as important in consensus decision making as it is in any other type of decision making. Being casual about the rules just makes a mess.

Consensus for Enduring Decisions....Only

In principle, consensus among the whole group is worth the effort for decisions intended to transcend generations. Consensus is achieved when every member of the group understands and consents to the same thing. It is much more arduous to make consensus decisions than it is to make majority-rule decisions or executive decisions. However, because of full understanding and consent among all members, consensus decisions are much more likely to last. When there is real consensus about a decision, there is no disgruntled minority working to change it later.

For a board of directors deciding its mission, values, or high-level policies – things intended to endure for future generations of board members – taking the time to develop consensus among all members is worth the effort. Deciding what the board will have for lunch – a decision that lasts only through dessert – consensus is not worth the effort.

Practical Tip: For every decision, consider how long it is expected to last and choose an appropriate method. Be deliberate about using consensus for some things, majority vote for other things, and delegate the short-order things to individuals, perhaps staff. We let a few of the members make short-term decisions on behalf of all the members because we trust they will be in keeping with long-term decisions decided by consensus of all the members.

Decide How to Decide

In principle, when parties cannot agree on an issue the next peaceful step is for them to decide how they are going to decide the issue. For instance, "We can't agree on the floor plan for the new building, so we're going to spend time on this at our next meeting, hear both sides, and vote. All okay with that?" If everyone can agree on HOW the thorny issue will be decided, that is progress toward agreement. When we send something to a committee or say something like, "Let's ask _____ and let her decide," we are making a decision about how to decide.

When diplomats or politicians spend time on meeting arrangements, seating plans, and the details of meeting agendas – the conditions under which the parties agree to meet – they are really deciding how they will decide. They are building agreement.

Practical Tip: When it seems like you are stuck and cannot decide something, at least decide how you will decide. Name a next step that moves in the direction of eventual agreement. Make a plan for a future discussion and vote, send it to a small group or committee with a specific charge, or name a third party decider.

Define the Edges

In principle, the center of a circle is equidistant from all points on the perimeter. We need to know the edges to know the center. To know what is centrally acceptable to a group of decision-makers, it helps to know the outer limits of acceptability: what is unacceptable.

Practical Tip: Say wild ideas. Make bold proposals. Be provocative. Know that the group is actually well-served when someone responds, "Now that is going too far," or "That is stepping over the line." Like a flashlight on a dark basketball court, shine it all over to find the boundaries.

If you are having a hard time defining how something should be, work for awhile on defining how it should not be. Try stuff on so you know what does not fit. Explore side roads so you know which ones dead end. Work inward from what you know is out of bounds.

P.S. Do not be attached to clothes that don't fit or roads that go nowhere.

Demonstrate Listening

In principle, peace comes through shared understanding and shared understanding comes through listening. If you hear things incorrectly, or not at all, you are likely to proceed on false assumptions which are likely to give way later and cause conflict. The best way to ensure good listening is to demonstrate it.

Practical Tip: Are you listening? Prove it. After you have heard someone say something, demonstrate to them that you heard them and understood what they said. Saying "I understand" is not a demonstration. (1) As you listen, show that you are paying attention with silent expressions and perhaps an encouraging word or two; (2) After hearing, reflect back what you heard. Ideally, repeat the main points, use a mix of the actual words they used and some of your own words, and try to name their feelings. Like, "My, that must have made you feel _____." Let them judge if you got it right. If you missed, no problem; try different words and talk it through until you "get it," and they agree that you get it.

The ultimate demonstration: act in ways that prove that you listened and understood.

Direction More Important Than Pace

In principle, moving quickly often seems like a good idea; but moving quickly in the wrong direction simply gets you to the wrong place fast. Most groups have a high need for quick achievement. We have all heard someone say, "Enough talk, let's just do something!" And we have all seen groups charge off quickly and with much enthusiasm…in the wrong direction.

Practical Tip: Even when under pressure to accomplish something in a hurry, resist the temptation to achieve a quick, although shabby, result. Quality group decisions, like anything of quality, require up front investment. Determine your objective before springing into action. Spend some time planning. Read the directions. Check out the map. As Bob Dylan says in Hard Rain, "I know my song well before I start singing."

No matter how slow you go, if you are headed in the right direction you might eventually get there.

Do What Say

In principle, trust grows from the link between what is said and what is done. When you are in a meeting and you say that you will do something, and then you don't, people trust you less. Sometimes the problem is not that you just couldn't get to the thing you said you would do, it is that you did not speak truth when you volunteered. Often the error is not in the "not doing," it is in the "saying" in the first place.

Practical Tip: Before you publicly (in a meeting, for instance) volunteer for anything, consider the commitment you are making. For every commitment made write something down, either on your calendar or on a to-do list. Do not just say "I'll do this or that" because it sounds good in the moment. Words without action are just words; and it is action that builds trust.

Fertile Soil Helps Creativity

In principle, good group decisions are creations. Creativity comes from putting together two or more things, events, ideas. Germination leads to new creations. Like water with a poppy seed, fertile soil facilitates and supports the interaction. Fertility helps creativity.

Practical Tip: Make your decision making environment "fertile." By design of meetings and communications, facilitate the interaction of multiple ideas. Make a culture of support and nurturing for new ideas. This might be done via ground rules or operating norms. Be consistent in their application. Uphold and stand by your ground rules in all situations. Deliberately attend to and nurture the environment in which you are trying to grow.

Freedom of Speech

In principle, in order to make good group decisions we need to hear all perspectives. We need be able to openly disagree with respect and civility. We need to have the courage to speak what is on our minds and hearts even in the face of opposition. When a group's culture makes it "not okay" to voice certain views, or when participants feel intimidated about sharing, those suppressed viewpoints do not go away; they just fester and turn into conflict later.

Practical Tip: Help create a group culture that encourages open sharing of all points of view. Offer encouragement and support to those who express minority opinions, even if you disagree. Stand tall and speak your own truth, and be genuinely open to considering others.

Expressing our differing opinions gives us a chance to understand each other better, talk, and inch toward resolution. When opinions are suppressed it might appear peaceful in the short run, but it inches us toward conflict over the long run.

Good in Everyone

In principle, the chances of making good group decisions are greatly increased if all the participants believe there is good in everyone. We are more likely to do well if we look for the best in each other. For some, believing that there is good in every person is a moral conviction. For others, seeking and bringing out the best in people is just plain practical.

Practical Tip: Act as if there is good in everyone, even when it is not apparent. Treat every person along your path as if they are special. If you believe in God, act as if there is that of God in every person.

To act this way is to give the benefit of the doubt. It is to assume best intentions. It is to be attentive, respectful, supportive, and encouraging. When you look for the best in people rather than the worst, it makes them want to be with you and work with you. When a group is relentlessly seeking out the best from within each person, people give their best to the group and great things are achieved.

Good Information Makes Decisions Self-Evident

In principle, there are basically three ways to influence the choices people make. You can regulate what people cannot do and punish violations. You can offer incentives to encourage certain choices. Third, you can provide accurate information that rings so true it compels good choices.

If you believe that for the most part people want to do the right thing, the most effective and peaceful method of influencing good decisions is to provide good information so "the right thing" becomes self-evident.

For example, historically Maine has had one of the highest teen smoking rates in the nation. We have made laws against teen smoking and imposed punishments for violations. We have placed incentives against smoking such as high taxes on cigarettes. These methods have not worked very well. Only recently have we seen the rate dramatically decline and it is because we launched an information campaign that has made clear the detrimental health effects of cigarette smoking. We have provided good information on TV and radio. For all those that "want to do the right thing," it has been clear what that is.

Practical Tip: Provide all decision makers with the best possible information about the issue being considered. Good, truthful information is terribly compelling. Actually, good information is the only thing that is truly compelling and results in good, sustainable decisions.

Gratitude

In principle, gratitude is all about attitude. Gratitude is a choice we make to see good in ourselves, our situation, and the people around us.

Discontent arises in me when there is a gap between what I have and what I want. When the gap is large I am apt to try to and close it by getting what I want. Advertisers know this so they breed discontent. They try to persuade me that what I have is not good enough and if I just had more and better stuff, I would be happy. Similarly, I am sometimes seduced into thinking that people around me are not good enough and that if they would just change their behaviors I would be happy.

It is okay to want things to be better, but it is not okay to put down ourselves, our situation, or our group in order to justify selfish behavior. A person lacking gratitude is likely to be a drag on good group decisions.

Sometimes getting what we want leads to happiness, but the surer way to close the gap of discontent is to look with gratitude upon that which we already have.

Practical Tip: Take stock of what you have and see the good in yourself, your situation, and your group. Imagine how things could be worse. Reach out and help someone less fortunate. Say thank you.

Ground Rules

In principle, when everybody understands and plays by the same rules the experience is much more likely to be fun and rewarding, rather than if people make up or assume their own rules and not everyone understands the rules. Like playground rules posted on a fence, meeting ground rules encourage that we play safe, have fun, and include everyone. Group decision making is more efficient and achieves better results when we have shared expectations of each other.

Practical Tip: Establish meeting ground rules at the start of every meeting, a simple list of ten or fewer statements about how you all agree to behave in the meeting. The group might make a list from scratch or might discuss and revise a list proposed by the facilitator. Many groups use the same set of ground rules meeting after meeting. All participants should be watchful for compliance with the ground rules and politely point out violations. Review the ground rules regularly and do not hesitate to make additions or changes. Make sure new people understand the ground rules.

Head, Heart, and Hands....All Three

In principle, if we want our group decisions to be creative, that is, result in new and better ways of doing things, we need to draw on all our resources and blend them in new ways. Typical meetings are structured to put our heads together, and indeed, our knowledge and ideas are a tremendous resource. But we have more. Why not go further and put our hearts together; share our feelings, stories, fears, and passions? Further still, why not put our hands together and do actual, physical activities as a group? In principle, a group decision process that includes intellectual exchange, sharing from the heart, and hands-on physical activity is most likely to yield creative results.

Practical Tip: Do not just do brainstorming, try heartstorming also. Do not just sit and talk about stuff together, get up and do stuff together, with your hands. If you want truly creative group decisions, share ideas, feelings, and activities....all three.

Humility

In principle, groups make their best decisions when no single person knows what is best for the group. There is a sign in a meeting room that I know of: "No one in this room is smarter than all of us." When I go into a meeting already sure of what the outcome should be I am apt to focus on getting my way rather than on what is best for the group as a whole. Knowing in advance how things should be closes off the potential of things being better than I can imagine.

Practical Tip: At the start of every meeting, say to yourself: "I do not know what is best for the group." Begin with an open mind and remain open-minded as long as possible. Maximize the value of your contributions by giving up ownership of them. Release the need to take credit and the need to be a victim. Simply play your right-sized part as best you can and watch the group's best unfold.

If It Fits In My Head, It Is Probably Too Small

In principle, big ideas are always the result of putting our heads together. Really big ideas are already out there in the heads of many people just waiting to be put together. Without sharing my ideas among fellows and without openness to new ideas, I am a prisoner of my own limitations incapable of more than I can imagine.

Practical Tip: The group is best served when participants are humble. You probably do not have all the best answers, and if you do, it is surely a small matter. Talk with others about your ideas and their ideas. Release your ideas, let them be criticized, and let them be built upon. Trust the wisdom of the group. It is okay to not understand everything; that it does not all fit in your head. Be open to ideas and achievements beyond your imagination.

If You Don't Have a Stake, Get Out of the Way

In principle, those who have a stake in the outcome, stakeholders, are the most appropriate participants in good group decisions. They stand to win, perhaps a lot, or lose a lot depending on the decision. In principle, those with the highest stakes tend to consider decisions most carefully. People who do not have a real stake may want to participate but may not consider issues deeply because they do not have to. Non-stakeholders are apt to give opinions based on shallow considerations, and those opinions can be in the way of the true stakeholders trying to achieve a good group decision.

Practical Tip: If you do not have a real stake in the decision, do not weigh in on the discussion. If you are about to say a sentence that begins something like, "Well I really don't care either way, but....," or "It doesn't matter to me, but....," consider saying nothing instead.

Interests Rather Than Positions

In principle, when someone comes into a meeting or a negotiation with an already-established position, it limits prospects for creative, innovative, win-win solutions. When I state my position on an issue early in the discussion, my focus thereafter becomes defending my position and trying to persuade others to agree with it. I might even get side-tracked into defending my pride rather than considering what is best for the group.

On the other hand, if I am able to speak clearly about my interests (what I would like to get out of the issue without attachment to a particular way of getting it), and I am able to listen openly to others' interests, we have a much better chance of all getting what we want.

— Good Question!

Practical Tip: Focus first on what you really want rather than how to get it. If you are leaning toward a particular solution, peel back a layer, dig a bit deeper, and ask, "What desire in me does this solution attempt to satisfy?" Ask yourself, "What is my fundamental interest here?" Identify what you are really interested in, give it words, and speak the words to others. Listen carefully to their words about their interests. As a group, hear and understand all interests before crafting solutions.

Positions spoken early invite argument. Interests spoken clearly invite win-win, creative solutions.

Dialogue & "Suspend" rather than "Defend"

Kindness

In principle, it's better to be kind than to be right. The ego in me wants me to be right. The peace seeker in me wants me to be kind. The word "kind" is related to the word "kin." They both come from the same root "kinn" meaning "family." To be kind is to treat people like family; as if we were intimately connected over time.

Practical Tip: To contribute to good group decisions, feed the peace seeker within, keep the ego in check, and strive for kindness. Take more interest in healthy relations with fellow decision makers over the long run than in getting your way in the short run. Give unconditionally without expectation of return, free of strings. True kindness is not only free, it's priceless.

Last Minute Decision Making

In principle, the more information we have about something the better decision we are likely to make. We are likely to have the most information at the last minute. Deciding more than we really need to at any given moment can cause regrets later.

Practical Tip: Before you start making decisions, think about the order of decisions. What needs to get decided first? What next? What can wait? Break decisions up into pieces if possible, and if there is anything to be gained by waiting to decide a piece (like more people getting more information), wait. Establish a date certain for deciding each piece.

The last minute, although potentially stressful, is often the optimum time for good group decisions. "I love the last minute," I once heard someone say. "If it weren't for the last minute a lot of stuff wouldn't get done."

Listen

In principle, just because a person is talking does not necessarily mean they are contributing, or that they are the only one contributing. Most of the time in a group decision setting, listening is the best contribution we can make. It is through listening, not talking, that we develop understanding, compassion, and creative solutions.

Practical Tip: Bite your tongue, cool your jets. To listen, do not talk. Do not be distracted by planning your talk.

If I let you talk first while I listen, it gives me some practical advantages. First, to hear where you are coming from helps me choose my words. You have likely provided me some new information that I can incorporate. Second, once you have your words out you are more likely to be open to hearing mine. Third, not talking gives me time to listen within. I help the group's decision process when I consider my inner thoughts, how I really feel about something, so that when my words are spoken they are aligned with inner truth.

Love

In principal, it is love that truly changes hearts and transforms people, not power or rules. It is love that compels sustained changes in behavior, not oaths or doctrines. It is love that provides a willingness to give; and it is love that helps us accept, let go, and find peace.

Most group decision making models encourage that we not include love in the mix. We are supposed to be objective, rational, and unemotional. This works well on the field of battle when the goal is to beat the other guys, but it does not work well when we are trying to find win-win, peaceful solutions. Peace asks us to love our neighbors.

Practical Tip: It is okay to allow love into your group decision making. This means encouraging passion...and compassion. It means treating everyone as a valued contributor, and no one as an enemy. It means making decisions not just with your head, but also with your heart. It means paying attention not only to the best available knowledge, but to wisdom. I once heard someone say, "Wisdom equals knowledge plus love."

Make Others Look Good

In principle, a good team is a group of people who try to make each other look good. Harry Truman said, "It is amazing what you can accomplish if you do not care who gets the credit." Similarly, we can spend huge amounts of energy caring about who gets the blame. To make good group decisions, we support each other going forward and we give credit for success to the group.

Practical Tip: Give your ideas and efforts to the group, without conditions, without lingering ownership. Show public appreciation for others in your group. Own your share of things gone wrong and share credit with others for things gone right.

More Wagging, Less Barking

In principle, you know when a dog is happy to see you and when not. People wag and bark too, in different ways. When two dogs approach each other wagging, expecting friendship, the outcome is almost always good. When one or more dogs is barking, it is hard to have a good outcome, hard to make good group decisions.

Practical Tip: Approach people wagging, expecting good things. Carry a sunny disposition. Look for the good in every person and in every situation...and let your optimism show. Wag more. Bark less.

My First Thought is Probably Not My Best

In principle, my initial reaction, my first thought, is very rarely my best. Often my first thought is absurd and shows me how NOT to react. Like first brush strokes on a canvas, first thoughts provide a starting place for more refined thoughts, for subsequent brush strokes. First thoughts, like initial brush strokes, are rarely worth sharing. In fact, sharing first thoughts can be deeply counter-productive to good group decisions.

Practical Tip: Just because you think something doesn't mean you have to say it, or act on it. When you share first thoughts you run a substantial risk of offending others, saying things you will regret, and requiring the group to spend time on issues which turn out to be a waste of time. Best to sit with your thoughts until a clear picture emerges of what you want to say.

Name Leads

In principle, whenever a group identifies something that needs to be done, it helps to name a "lead;" that is, the person responsible for taking the next step. If a new committee is formed, who is responsible for convening the first meeting? If more information about something is needed, who will actually gather it and report back to the group? Things for which no one is directly responsible tend to get dropped. Naming a "go to" person (lead) for each thing lets everyone know who to call if they have a question about it. Being named lead on something gives me a sense of responsibility and compels me to do a good job.

Practical Tip: Before adjourning a meeting, make sure that a name is attached to every action item. Encourage people to take leads. If you believe something is important, consider taking the lead yourself. Do not assign the lead to someone who is not present without their permission. If an item arises for which no one is willing to take the lead, let it drop; this is a clear sign that there is not enough energy among the group to actually implement even though it "seems like a good idea." Groups are good at generating ideas, but individual leadership gets things done.

No Complaining Without Contribution

In principle: If I have not tried to make something better or if I am not willing to help make it better, I have no business complaining about it. Rather than stand outside the circle and complain about the decisions made by others, I do well to appreciate those who are willing to do the hard work of group decision making. In fact, complaining without contribution actually hurts good group decisions because it demoralizes current decision-makers and discourages potential new ones.

Practical Tip: If you are unhappy or disappointed with the decisions of your group (perhaps an organization you belong to or perhaps your government), before criticizing, first be grateful for the decision-makers' efforts. Second, try to understand their perspective, how it is different from your own, and why. Third, if your discontent is real and lasting, ask yourself, "What am I willing to do about it?" Ask yourself, "Am I willing to change my personal behavior in some way to make things better? Am I willing to somehow participate in the next round of decision making?"

A thoughtful, "I'm going to _____" followed up with action is always much more effective than a lazy, "You should _____," or "They should _____."

Not Her Fault, Her Type

In principle, we each have a personality type, hardwired into us, not likely to change. There are many methods of assessing personality types, Myers-Briggs the most famous among them. Most assessments consist of a written test that reveals one's basic type. Categorizing people into four basic types has been going on since 400BC. Hippocrates called them the four temperaments. In medieval times they were called the four cardinal humors.

With a certain personality type come certain personality traits. Our type has to do with how we learn, how we act, how we perceive others and the world, and how some abilities come naturally to us and some don't.

Practical Tip: To help make good group decisions, keep in mind that people are different, not everyone is good at everything, and others see things differently than you, instinctively. When someone does not do something the way you would do it, figure it is not his intention to be difficult, he is just different.

That people are different from you is never their fault. Rather, it is their gift. Try to embrace and build on the gifts of others, and your own.

Outside Issues

In principle, disagreements are generally because of: misunderstandings, differing values, or outside issues. Misunderstandings and differing values can generally be resolved within the group. When a disagreement is caused by an outside issue that has nothing to do with the issue at hand, then it must either be dealt with outside the group or someone might end up losing, and that might be okay.

An "outside issue" is a disagreement because of, for example, some incident between the parties that happened years ago and has never been dealt with, or because of a mental disorder such as an addiction which is warping someone's judgment or behavior. Or perhaps it is because of a misconception closely-held since childhood, or an unreasonable fear. Outside issues are usually personal and are often completely unrelated to the group's immediate business.

If an outside issue is in the way, agreement will only come if the issue is dealt with. If it is not dealt with and the disagreeing parties cannot let go, than the group might get paralyzed by an issue they have no ability to fix.

Practical Tip: Once you recognize that an outside issue is the cause of a disagreement, encourage the parties to deal with it outside the group. Perhaps therapy is called for, or mediation. If they are unwilling or unable, take a vote or hire an arbitrator or somehow otherwise resolve the issue even over objection. Losing is not always bad. Sometimes it is the only thing that will allow some people move forward. It is better that one or two people lose a single issue than the group as a whole gets stuck and unable to make progress.

Plan, Meet, Write-Up

In principle, the three fundamental steps that make a meeting great are to (1) plan what you are going to meet about, (2) actually meet according to the plan, and then (3) write up the meeting results.

Practical tip: In the case of an upcoming meeting, the meeting facilitator and/or group leaders should huddle in advance to be clear on the meeting objectives, agenda, roles, how it will be recorded, and logistics such as invitations, space, food, nametags, etc. Talk it through and plan out how each part of the meeting will work. Advance planning increases chances that you will have on hand the things you need for the meeting to go well and sharing the plan in advance increases chances that participants will come prepared and that their expectations will be on target.

Then, run the meeting according to plan (although always be prepared to be flexible and responsive to things unplanned). Meeting according to plan provides security for participants.

After, provide participants with a write-up that is more than a simple chronological transcript. Organize the thoughts and stories shared, name the themes discussed, and format the write-up so it is pleasant to read and easy to refer to later. In the write-up you can provide a logical organizational structure even if things seemed quite confusing during the actual meeting.

Do not skimp on the pre-planning or the post-write-up. These are the two things that often distinguish a great meeting from a mediocre one.

Pose Alternatives

In principle, considering alternative solutions makes for better decisions. Exploring alternatives either: (1) builds faith in the leading option (we get to see that the leading option really is the best among alternatives); (2) leads to a new, better solution; or (3) reveals that we do not have a clear handle on the problem (posing alternative solutions pushes us to clearly define the problem that we are trying to solve).

Practical Tip: Even when you think you have the right answer, pose alternatives. Consider, "What are some other ways to approach this? How else could we get the job done? How else could we solve the problem?" Be wildly creative. Be hypothetical. Like a child posing dolls or trucks, be imaginative. After you have posed and considered alternatives, then decide.

Putting People in Boxes is Not Okay

In principle, when we look at people in certain ways, place labels on them, or "put them in boxes," it limits what they have to offer. It is especially tempting to "contain" those who disagree with us. We are tempted to ignore our adversaries, work around them, wall them off, shut them down. These techniques might help us win as individuals, but they work against making good group decisions.

In principle, the best group decisions come when we genuinely consider ALL offerings, not just the ones we like. In fact, what makes group decisions better than individual decisions is the tension of initial disagreement.

Practical Tip: Muster the courage to really consider disagreement. Muster the discipline to work with people you do not like. Resist labels, walls, boxes and be open-minded to all offerings. When someone is placed in a box – silenced, contained, ignored – they add about as much value to the decision as, well...a cardboard box.

Reflective Pause

In principle, it is rarely beneficial to say the first thing that comes to mind. Just because I think or feel something does not mean I have to say it. Even when there is a sense of urgency; especially when there is a sense of urgency, I am better off if I take time to breathe, reflect, and consider my words before speaking them.

A reflective pause helps me avoid saying something I will later regret. When I say regretful things it causes unnecessary tension and potentially huge inefficiencies in my group.

Practical Tip: In a group setting, honor a moment of silence before and after each comment, like bookends. If tensions in a group are dangerously high, call for a break or a few moments of silence before proceeding. As a group participant, refrain from hasty reactions.

Thank God I have learned the value of placing a pause between receiving and reacting. I have seen how the peacefulness of one breath can avert a windstorm of trouble.

Resentments Have Roots in Expectations

In principle, when we have expectations of others that don't pan out it often leads to resentment, which often leads to brewing discontent or bubbling-over conflict. I have heard, "expectations are planned resentments." The surest way to avoid resentment is to not have expectations. When I fall into a victim role it is helpful to remember that rarely am I a victim of others and often I am a victim of my own expectations.

[handwritten annotation: Great reframe!]

Practical Tip: As a participant in good group decisions, try hard not to develop false expectations. Expect from people ONLY that to which they have specifically agreed, and even then keep in mind that most people are not capable of doing all that they agree to. Focus on the good things that your group and the people in it have done, and what they could do, rather than what they should do according to your expectations.

Rules First

In principle, it is best to make the rules before taking the field, before starting the meeting. When we decide HOW we are going to make decisions before we find ourselves in the tension of making them, it lowers our chances of conflict. It is much easier to establish proposal development steps and decision criteria in the hypothetical rather than when actually confronted with a real proposal and with real personalities. "We'll figure out the rules as we go," rarely turns out fair and often leads to conflict and resentment. Establishing rules of engagement beforehand lets everyone know what to expect, gives everyone equal opportunity to participate, and increases chances of creative, peaceful decisions.

use these on the flip charts!

Practical Tip: Before you get to the hard decisions, first establish who gets to vote and who does not, how proposals get developed and discussed, and norms of behavior for meetings. For most groups, such rules are embodied in bylaws and meeting ground rules. Imagine the tough situations before they arrive and decide in advance how they will be handled.

Establishing and enforcing rules does not limit creativity, but rather encourages it. Knowing what to expect gives us courage to fully participate.

Separate Inputs from Outcomes

In principle, groups make their most creative, win-win decisions when each participant puts in their personal best and no participant thinks they know best for the group. It works best when no single participant is working for a single, pre-determined outcome.

Practical Tip: Show up, pay attention, give your best, and let go of the outcome. Go into meetings well prepared, with an open mind, and a humble heart. Take full responsibility for playing your part as best you can and do not take full responsibility for how it all turns out.

Separate Process from Program

In principle, when group participants are allowed to manipulate the process to favor specific programs, it tilts power toward a few, limits creativity, and clogs efficiency. It is typical in Congress, state legislatures, and town governments, for instance, to spend a lot of time debating process issues, agenda setting, committee membership, and rules...often in order to influence the substance, or outcome.

To maximize efficiency, equality, and creativity, some groups hire a facilitator who works for the group as a whole and manages the process. This is like when sports teams agree to hire a referee so as NOT to spend time arguing the rules when time is precious, like in a game...or in a meeting.

Practical Tip: Separate process from program. Get a good facilitator to manage the process so all others can focus on program (the substance of your work). The facilitator may be from among the group and unpaid, but it is best if he or she does not have a stake in the outcome (the program) and can refrain from giving views. The participants should empower the facilitator as referee and thereafter focus on creative, win-win solutions.

Great!

Shared Expectations Minimize Conflicts

In principle, most conflicts are because of mismatched expectations. Where the expectations are really different the conflict can be really big. No one likes disappointment: when you think something is going to be one way, and then it changes. The best prevention is a shared expectation of how things are going to be, who is going to do what, and how things are going to work.

Practical Tip: Among two or more people with a shared task, figure out your shared expectations and write them down (or at least say them) so you can test your shared understanding. Contracts are shared expectations written down, so are ground rules, guidelines, and by laws. The process of writing these documents forces us to "out" our expectations and understand each other. If you do not take time to discuss expectations with those on who you plan to depend, best not to have any.

Shared Values

In principle, values are those things most important to us; the things we value. For most people, they are ideals, beliefs, rules to live by. We are generally drawn to be with people who share our values. At the core of every defined group of people are shared values.

Practical Tip: Discuss values as a group and make a written, short, agreed-to list of the values you have in common. Simply having a discussion about values helps a group to understand each other. Deciding which values you share defines your group and helps people decide to join the group. It also helps people to leave when they are not a good fit. A written list of shared values also serves as a "code of ethics," a place to turn for guidance when the decision making gets tough.

Shared values are the steadfast ground on which we stand when things are in turmoil. Shared values guide and hold us together.

Shared Vision Required

In principle, it is a shared vision that holds a group together; a common view of how people want things to be different in the future. If my opinion of how things should change does not overlap with yours, in at least a tiny way, we have no reason to work together. It may be that we disagree on specific approaches – how much money to spend, who to hire, when to do what – but for a good group decision to result we must have a shared vision of the outcome; where we are heading.

Practical Tip: Identify and write down what your group agrees on and what you all hope to achieve. For an established group this might be a mission statement, a vision statement, or a set of goals. For a one-time group (perhaps gathered at a public hearing, for instance), begin with a statement of why the group is gathered and make sure at the outset that everyone is there for the same purpose. Starting off knowing that there is something everyone agrees on helps later.

Speak Your Truth and Let Go of the Outcome

In principle, an extremely valuable contribution I can make to a group decision is to discern my own "truth" and share it with the group. Deep inside, what do I really feel? This requires me to cut through the clutter of all that is on my mind. Discerning my truth requires me to be in touch with my feelings and to be honest with myself. Sharing my truth requires courage. Protecting myself requires detachment from the outcome. How others react to my truth is not my responsibility.

Practical Tip: Speak what is on your heart rather than what is on your mind. Do not get mired in calculating the consequences. Speak your truth and let go of the outcome. One way to be sure you are speaking truth: say only what you feel. No one can argue with what you feel.

Once I was in a meeting and spoke my truth. Afterwards, I became terribly afraid of the consequences. I asked someone, "Did I say the right thing?" The response came without hesitation. "How could you not have?" they replied. "You spoke from your heart."

Straw Vote

In principle, the best group decisions are based on shared understanding of everyone's perspective, and the best way to get a quick read of where everyone stands is to take a straw vote. A straw vote is not a real vote; it does not count over the long run, like straw. Someone might say, "Let's just see how people feel about the latest idea. All those who tend to like it, show a thumb up. If you tend not to like it, show a thumb down. If you are neutral or undecided, show a horizontal thumb." Count the thumbs in the three categories. That is a straw vote.

It lets everyone in the group see, in a quick and general way, if "the latest idea" is worth more group time and energy. It also shows where the concerns are (the down thumbs) so the facilitator knows who to call on to hear concerns.

Some groups use color cards for straw votes. Some use high-tech remote key pads and the results are graphed instantly on a screen in front of the room. The most efficient groups use straw votes often and with ease.

Practical Tip: Do not hesitate to call for, or participate in, a straw vote. Before calling for a straw vote, make sure the question is clear and simple; you do not want to waste group time haggling about: "What are we voting on?" When calling for a straw vote, remind everyone that it does not count over the long run, that everyone has the right to change their mind later, and that it is simply a quick and blurry snapshot of how the group feels at this moment. Still, even a snapshot can be worth a thousand words.

Structure Sets You Free

In principle, decision making "structure" consists of things like rules, agendas, mandates, and plans; and when these things frame our choices it frees us to focus on the substance of our work. A third-grade teacher once explained that when she decides where the kids are to sit in the classroom this does not take away their freedom, but actually frees them from the burden of having to decide this for themselves (a potentially large burden for a third-grader). It frees them to focus on math, history, and writing rather than who to sit next to.

==Establishing a firm structure allows maximum creativity within the structure. Knowing there is a "container" provides safety and encourages risk-taking.== Lack of structure fosters anxiety and encourages caution. Lack of structure causes inefficiency; it requires a group to go over the same ground over and over again.

Practical Tip: Establish decision making rules in your group and make it someone's responsibility to enforce them; this frees everyone else from having to worry about that. Make sure everyone understands and agrees to the rules before you decide other things. When you have a complex decision ahead of your group, break it into pieces with a timeline for deciding each piece. Focus on one piece at a time. As you near decisions, narrow choices to a small number of alternatives. Be bold in enforcing your structure...and go wild within it.

Take a Step

In principle, we do not need to know the whole plan in order to take the next step. To avoid a stumble we do not need to see the whole path illuminated, just the next few feet. As if carrying a lantern through the dark, if I take just one step at a time more will be revealed. The light moves with me.

Practical Tip: Just because you cannot see how everything is going to work out, do not let that stop you from taking the next step. If your group seems stuck with uncertainty, ask "What do we need to know JUST to take the next step?" Let that be enough for now. Take a step. As an individual, let go of needing to know everything and trust that your lantern will see you through.

Talk or Listen

In principle, a simple but important decision I have to make every moment in a group is whether to open my mouth or to keep it shut; to talk or to listen. I contribute best to good group decisions if I set the default to "listen." After all, God gave me two open ears and one closeable mouth. I listen unless there are compelling reasons to talk, not vice versa.

Practical Tip: Listen most of the time and speak up only if: (1) you personally care about the issue and have a real stake in it; (2) you understand the issue enough to add useful, accurate information; (3) what you want to say has not already been said, even with different words, AND; (4) it is the right time for speaking on the issue. It is also okay to talk if you are simply compelled by a voice within to share your feelings. If each of the four conditions is met or if you have strong feelings screaming to be shared, then yes! Please speak up. The group will benefit from your words. Otherwise, best to listen.

Understand First

In principle, understanding is that upon which we stand. It is the basis for all our beliefs and actions, like a foundation. All we do and say is based upon our understanding of the situation. We do best to make sure we fully understand before judging and before acting.

Practical Tip: Be aware about crossing the line between understanding the situation and solving the problem. In a conversation, ask questions before offering advice. In a meeting, be sure you fully understand the proposal before giving your opinions about it. Ninety percent of all disagreements are due to misunderstandings, and disagreements often disappear when we take the time to understand where each other are coming from.

How things look always depends on where you sit. Misunderstandings, presumptions, and premature judgments almost always result in bad decisions. Shared understanding is the basis for good group decisions.

Understanding and Trust, Both Required

In principle, when making good group decisions we try to get all the facts and fully understand before deciding. But it is impossible to understand every detail, every nuance, every possibility, and that's where trust takes over. We work to understand as much as we can, but at some point we just need to trust our intuition, other people, and/or the process.

For the rational person, the path to truth is paved mostly with understanding, with a bit of trust at the end. For the intuitive person, the path to truth begins with a bit of understanding and then trust paves most of the way. For all of us, truly good decisions require some combination of understanding and trust.

Practical Tip: Work on both understanding and trust. Understand: gather the facts, hear all perspectives, review best practices, and apply rigorous scientific methodology. At the same time, build trust: do things together, eat together, support each other through hardships, share stories and photos of your loved ones. Answer as many questions as you can but at some point you have to decide even without every answer…and it comes down to trust.

Us Over Me

In principle, the most likely path for a group to be highly productive, happy, and endure over generations is for individuals to put group needs over individual needs. In western culture we receive many messages that encourage us to put self first, the most likely path to short term gain. In a "Me First" culture, individuals prevail but groups, communities, and species die. Good group decisions require a culture of "Us Over Me."

Practical Tip: In group decision making, be thoughtful about how a decision affects the group as a whole. Whatever would be best for the group, work on that path and vote that way. Discuss it as a group and see if "Us Over Me" is a shared value. Consider wide impacts of decisions to other communities and into the future. Apply humility.

What's the Problem?

In principle, more often than not, a group will develop a great solution to the wrong problem. Before proceeding with a solution we need to see that it is aimed squarely at the problem and to do that we need to bring the problem into focus. Taking time to define the problem may seem like "unnecessary process" in the short term, but can save huge amounts of time and energy over the long run. Defining the problem as a group also checks our shared expectations. It helps me decide, "Is this something in which I want to participate?"

Practical Tip: Before discussing solutions, discuss the problem. What are you trying to fix? What is the specific scope of the problem that you are willing to take on? How would you know if the problem was fixed? Are you the right group to fix it?

On paper, write something like, "The problem is that _____." It could be a sentence or it could be a paragraph. Refrain from discussing solutions until you have agreement on the problem statement. Make sure that all those working on the problem are aware of the written problem statement and agree with it. Before firing off solutions, make sure the problem is in focus.

Write On the Walls

In principle, good group decisions stem from shared understanding, and shared understanding comes from reading off the same page. To see things the same way, write words for everyone to see.

And, good group decisions stem from all views being heard. The best way for someone to feel heard is for their view to get written for everyone to see.

Practical Tip: For every group meeting, have on hand the ability to write words for everyone to see. Markers and a flip chart work well and many groups these days use a laptop and projector. There are many creative ways.

When people make comments, paraphrase them on the chart or the screen. The words do not need to be perfect, but "representative" of the view being expressed. When it seems like the group is agreeing to something, write words to represent the agreement. Make sure everyone understands and accepts the representative words.

Writing public words that represent viewpoints and agreements is a learned skill and requires focused effort. When done well it leads to shared understanding and individual empowerment: two key building blocks of good group decisions.

Written Words Clarify

In principle, the value of written words is that they can be seen by several people simultaneously, and over time. Further, the process of choosing words helps us be sure we understand. Writing and agreeing on words together breeds shared understanding. Without a written record to underpin the understanding or agreement, you can count on ever changing accounts of what happened.

Practical Tip: When making good group decisions, have large paper on hand for all to see, or a computer screen projected on the wall. The paper or screen serves as a blank canvas for shared creation. To check for shared understanding or agreement, take your best shot at the right words and write them for all to see. Discuss the words and change the words until there is general agreement that they reflect the sense of the group. Writing and agreeing on words is harder than nodding heads to spoken comments, but it saves time and conflict over the long run.

Our Licensing Agreement with You

You are free to:

- copy, distribute, display, and perform this work
- make derivative works
- make commercial use of this work

Under the following conditions:

Attribution. You must attribute the work in the manner specified by the author or licensor; that is, the names "Freshley" or "Good Group Decisions" must appear on every page and with every quote.

Share Alike. If you alter, transform, or build upon this work, you may distribute the resulting work only under a license identical to this one.

For any reuse or distribution, you must make clear to others the license terms of this work.

Any of these conditions can be waived if you get permission from the copyright holder, Craig Freshley.

Your fair use and other rights are in no way affected by the above.

This license agreement is based on Creative Commons License Agreement: Attribution-ShareAlike, 2.5. Learn more at www.CreativeCommons.org.

Order More Copies of This Book

This book is published in two formats: as an e-book and as a paperback. Both formats are available at our website.

E-book

The electronic version of this book, a portable document format (pdf) file, is free and available for download at www.GoodGroupDecisions.com.

5"x 8" Paperback

If you are planning to download and then print this 80-page book on your computer printer, please consider paying a few dollars and let us send you a nicely bound paperback. Or buy it at your local book store. Your printer ink, paper, and effort would cost you a few dollars anyway.

Order the paperback through your local bookstore or at our website: www.GoodGroupDecisions.com.

At our website, we offer significant volume discounts for multiple copies.

Subscribe to Tips

New Tips are sent to subscribers by e-mail every two weeks at no charge. Each one is designed to print on a single page. They contain no advertising.

Sign up for a subscription at www.GoodGroupDecisions.com. We do not share the e-mail list with anyone and we never add anyone to the list unless they ask us to. Each subscriber proactively signs up. Subscriptions are free.

About our Company

Our company is growing fast, a reflection of growing interest in collaborative-style decisions, we hope.

We have been a consulting company for three years and recently became a publisher. As consultants, we have facilitated hundreds of meetings and written dozens of public policy reports. All our past and present clients are described at our website.

Also at our website you can download free handouts, check out training workshops, and learn about our staff and associates.

Also, check out our mission, values, and our 1% for the Earth policy.

www.GoodGroupDecisions.com

Tips to make Good Group Decisions, Volume 1 *Freshley*

Printed in the United States
71126LV00001B/121-219